Succeed as a
New Manager

How to inspire your team
and be a great boss

A & C Black • London

Revised edition first published in Great Britain 2009

A & C Black Publishers Ltd
36 Soho Square, London W1D 3QY
www.acblack.com

A CIP record for this book is available from the British Library.

ISBN: 9–781–4081–1189–5

This book is produced using paper that is made from wood grown
in managed, sustainable forests. It is natural, renewable and
recyclable. The logging and manufacturing processes conform to
the environmental regulations of the country of origin.

Design by Fiona Pike, Pike Design, Winchester
Typeset by RefineCatch Ltd, Bungay, Suffolk
Printed in Spain by GraphyCems

Contents

How do you rate as a new manager?

Answer the questions and work out your score, then read the guidance points.

How do you feel about your new role?
a) Terrified!
b) Excited–I feel ready for my new role.
c) Very confident; I've waited a long time for this.

Have you made any decisions about your management style?
a) I don't plan on acting any differently.
b) I'll be friendly and approachable.
c) I'll treat colleagues very differently as they will be working *for* me, not with me.

How do you feel about managing people older than you?
a) I worry about my lack of experience.
b) I don't see that age is an issue.
c) It's not a problem.

Be truthful! Out of 10, how do you rate your listening skills?
a) 4–6
b) 7–10
c) 1–3

How often do you say 'thank you'?

a) Too much!

b) Regularly.

c) Not very often.

What is your view on conflict?

a) I avoid it if at all possible.

b) Sometimes it's unavoidable.

c) I don't have a problem with it!

Which of the below is closest to your style of communication?

a) Passive.

b) Assertive.

c) Aggressive.

How do you view delegation?

a) I see it as laziness. If a job comes to you, you should deal with it yourself.

b) An important process for developing both yourself and your staff.

c) Very handy–if you don't want to do something, pass it on!

How do you feel about your managers?

a) I worry that they don't think much of me.

b) I respect their experience. We're all on the same team.

c) I don't think much of them, so try to avoid them and get on with my job.

a = 1, b = 2, and c = 3.

Now add up your scores.

■**9–14:** Now you have had the good news it's important to build up your confidence, reminding yourself that your company has chosen to promote you. If they believe in you there's no reason why you shouldn't! Read chapter **1** to give you a head start. To avoid getting bogged down in detail, you mustn't be afraid to delegate–chapter **5** will give you some pointers, and chapter **7** will help you manage your personal workload.

■**15–21:** You clearly have a balanced approach to your new role, but don't underestimate the change this will cause in your working relationships. Remember to keep a professional distance. Chapters **3** and **4** will help you to feel at home as a manager. Building teams is a new skill for you to learn–read all about it in chapter **2**.

■**22–27:** Remember that overconfidence can be a problem too! You are in danger of damaging relationships through your perceived arrogance. Listening and 'bonding' are very important skills for managers–read chapters **4** and **6** for advice on positive management.

Whatever your score, remember that as your role grows so should your contacts list. Chapter **8** will help you build a network of mutually valuable contacts.

Settling into your new job

Congratulations! Your promotion campaign has been successful and you're now a manager. You're likely to be responsible for managing a team of up to 15 people, either in a company you already work for, or in a new organisation. This is obviously very exciting for you, though you may feel a bit daunted at the prospect, especially if you were previously a member of the team you will now be managing.

However, provided you follow a few basic rules, there is no reason why such fears can't easily be overcome, and your new role will give you excellent scope to stretch your wings and fulfil your potential. This chapter will give you these basic rules and help to smooth the path forward into this new phase of your working life.

Step one: Think about some key questions

I   I'm worried I might not be up to the job. How can I overcome my nerves?

It's only natural to have some feelings along these lines, and most people do when faced with a new challenge. Try to keep your worries under control, though, as a crisis of confidence may affect your chance of success. Keep positive and remind yourself of your skills and competence to do the job—after all, the company has recognised them, otherwise you wouldn't have been offered the role! Look after your health too: make sure you get plenty of sleep and exercise, so you feel fighting fit and ready to take on anything.

2 Is it likely that my new job will affect my home life?

Almost certainly, yes. Moving into any new job can be stressful, and even more so when new or extra levels of responsibility are involved. The trick is to make sure you're prepared for it, and face the fact that your life may be more demanding than ever before. Talk this over with your family and friends at an early stage; it will be a huge help if they are ready to lend their support while you get to grips with your new role, and also keep 'home' distractions to a minimum as you're settling in so that you can focus.

3 Will I need to change my persona at work?

No, not essentially, but you may need to adjust your attitude and the way you think about your job. A lot of management is about standing back from the detail and seeing the 'big picture' of what is happening so that you can make strategic decisions about how to act. Rather than getting involved in the nitty-gritty of individual tasks (as you may have done as a team member), try to take an objective overview. If you can learn to see the wood for the trees, you'll naturally behave in a way that suits the circumstances.

Step two: Research and plan your new job

First things first: if you're moving to a new company to take up your job, find out everything possible about it, the department or section you'll be in, the job itself, and anything else you can think of.

If you're moving up the ranks at your current place of work, you'll know much of this already, but, whatever the situation, don't prejudge what you're going to find and don't be bound by what you've done before or how any of your previous employers operated.

From all this information, try to form at least a tentative plan in advance—it's much harder to do this once you're in the post. For example, what do you want to achieve? How might you need to develop yourself to match the new demands? Think honestly about your strengths and weaknesses: how can you use your qualities and experience to their best advantage and compensate for your limitations?

Step three: Engage with your team

Once you start your new job, make this your first priority. You need to know:

- the purpose of your department, team, or unit and its goals
- the work being done
- the current state of play
- any customer expectations that need to be met

Get all your team members together as soon as possible to introduce yourself, and then arrange meetings with each of them individually. Keep these meetings as friendly and informal as you can, but allow a generous amount of time and plan some kind of framework for the discussion. Listen carefully to what people have to say, and get information about them as individuals. Most importantly, ask each person the question: what should I do or not do to help you perform your job effectively?

TOP TIP

Listening—and tuning in properly—to your team's concerns is a key part of your early days in a new job. That doesn't mean for a moment that you should promise them the moon, but simply that you'll be in a much better position to represent those concerns to your own managers. You need to be able to fight your team's corner.

Step four: Plan some 'quick wins'

Next, plan a few targets that you can hit quickly and easily, all of which will help you to feel more at home and on top of things. Achieving these also eases the pressure you feel to perform and create a positive first impression and begins the relationship-building process. Quick wins might include things like familiarising yourself with systems or ways of working if you're new to the company (for example, the internal e-mail system); setting up an early discussion with your line manager, arranging introductory meetings with suppliers or customers (external and internal), or even taking your team to the pub one lunchtime.

Step five: Clarify what expectations others have of you

You may be lucky enough to have been given a detailed job description, but the chances are there are still large gaps in your understanding of the task and priorities, what is or isn't acceptable in the new environment, and on what criteria you will be judged by your boss, peers, customers, and others. Don't be afraid to ask a lot of questions to clarify these issues, and then be very honest with yourself. Can you meet these standards? If not, what might you need to do? Who could help, and what might the price be?

The perils of the 'new broom' syndrome

While you'll be keen to get going in your new role and make your mark, do tread carefully—at least to start with. Don't assume that your new team will welcome your style or your ideas with open arms, even if your predecessor was unpopular. Before you can count on their support and co-operation, they need to feel that they can trust you and that you respect what they've been doing previously.

Above all, don't depart too dramatically and quickly from established practice: even if you're desperate to change 'the way things are done around here', people are much less likely to throw their hands up in horror if you tackle

things gradually. That doesn't mean that you do nothing,
simply that you filter in new ideas and ways of working bit
by bit.

Step six: Show your commitment to individual development

From your initial meetings with your team, you will know
what their individual aspirations and hopes are for their jobs
going forward. Follow up by setting a code of management
practice that you tell all team members about, and then
follow it rigorously. This code might include commitments to
assess training needs, to hold regular team meetings and
one-to-one sessions, to set specific goals, and to evaluate
performance against these goals.

Support this code by the way you yourself behave towards
team members. Make a point of appreciating extra time and
effort that people put in, listen properly to what they say, and
be generous in your praise of their good qualities or
achievements. The point is, that by demonstrating to your
team that you as their manager are on their side and will do
everything in your power to support them, you will gain their
trust and acceptance, and the performance of the whole
team will be greatly enhanced.

Step seven: Lead by example

A good manager is also a role model, so it almost goes without saying that you must set an example for how you want your team members to behave. Lead by involving people in establishing group objectives, setting standards, and achieving deadlines, and demonstrate your own strong personal commitment to achieving the team's goals. Set an

---

TOP TIP

In most workplaces, there's nearly always someone who is a nightmare to work with. Before you were a manager, if you had a troublesome colleague you may have let off steam about him or her to a friend in the office. Being a boss doesn't mean you have to be a saint, clearly, but it does mean that you have to be extremely careful about what you say about colleagues and to whom. Even if you feel like screaming, don't commit any derogatory comments about a colleague to e-mail: it's all too easy to inadvertently send them to the wrong person. Also be careful about conversations you have in the office— you could be overheard. Use your common sense and, if you can, wait until you get home and unburden yourself to someone completely outside of your work life: your partner, friends, family members, or pet!
